PETROLEUM
gas, oil and asphalt

IRVING ADLER
illustrated by Peggy Adler

The John Day Company • *New York*

THE REASON WHY SERIES

Library of Congress Cataloging in Publication Data
Adler, Irving. Petroleum. (His The Reason why books) Includes index.
SUMMARY: Discusses the different kinds of oil, how they are found and recovered, their uses, and the problems of pollution, oil conservation, and oil shortage.
1. Petroleum—Juvenile literature. [1. Petroleum]
I. Alder, Peggy, ill. II. Title.
TN870.A247   1975   553'.28   75-2431
ISBN 0-381-99624-7RB

10 9 8 7 6 5 4 3 2 1

Contents

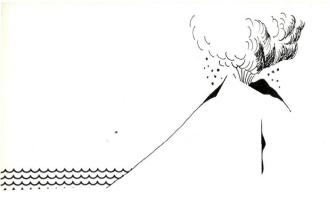

Petroleum

Petroleum comes from the ground. It is found in many parts of the world.

We drill wells for it on land and under the sea.

We burn it to produce energy. We change it chemically to make such different things as paint, phonograph records, explosives, fibers, antifreeze and food containers.

It took millions of years to make petroleum. It has been used in large amounts for only about one hundred years. It will

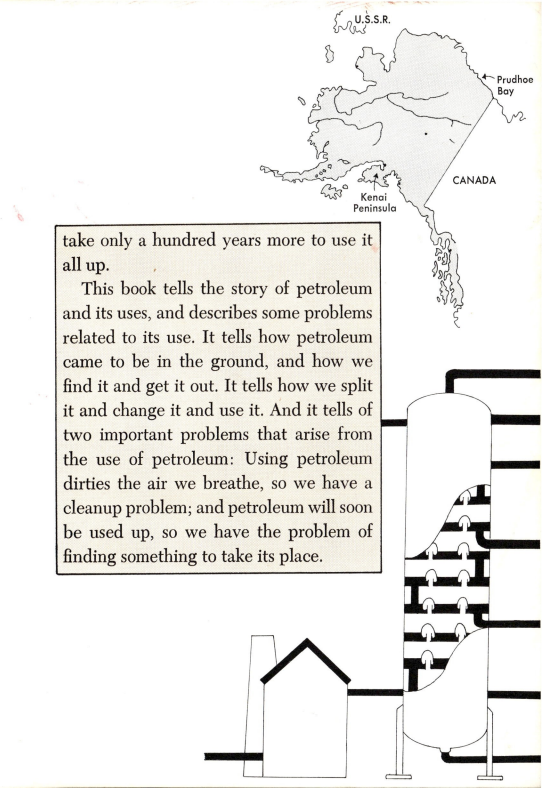

take only a hundred years more to use it all up.

This book tells the story of petroleum and its uses, and describes some problems related to its use. It tells how petroleum came to be in the ground, and how we find it and get it out. It tells how we split it and change it and use it. And it tells of two important problems that arise from the use of petroleum: Using petroleum dirties the air we breathe, so we have a cleanup problem; and petroleum will soon be used up, so we have the problem of finding something to take its place.

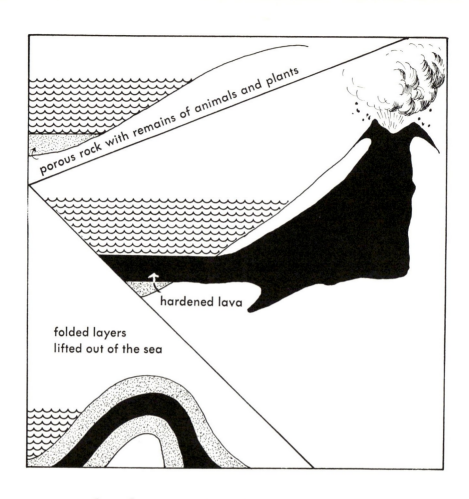

porous rock with remains of animals and plants

hardened lava

folded layers
lifted out of the sea

Oil in the Ground, and How It Got There

The word *petroleum* means *rock oil*. It comes from two Latin words, *petra* (rock) and *oleum* (oil), and refers to oil and oily substances that are found in the ground. Petroleum may be a gas, called *natural gas*, or a liquid, called *crude oil*, or a solid substance, called *asphalt*.

Asphalt is found on the surface of the earth in some places, in asphalt lakes like Pitch Lake in Trinidad, West Indies, or the asphalt pit in Hancock Park near Los Angeles, California. Crude oil and natural gas have also been found occasionally at the surface, where they seep or flow out of the ground. However, most crude oil and natural gas are deep under the ground, and wells have to be drilled to bring them to the surface.

Petroleum was formed millions of years ago from the bodies of small animals and plants that lived and died in ancient seas. The bodies fell to the sea floor, where they were covered by mud and sand carried to the sea by ancient rivers. The mud and sand, pressed by their own weight and the weight of the sea, and cemented by chemicals in the seawater, hardened to form *porous* rocks (rocks with many small spaces in them), like *shale, sandstone* and *limestone*. The bodies, trapped in the rock, decayed only partly and became petroleum. Many layers of these porous rocks were formed, one on top of the other. Sandwiched in among them were also nonporous rocks, formed by the cooling of lava that flowed out of volcanoes. Movements of the earth's surface folded these layers of rock and lifted many of them out of the sea.

Early Discovery and Uses

People have known about petroleum and some of its uses since ancient times. As far back as six thousand years ago, asphalt and oil were used in Mesopotamia, located in the region now known as Iraq. When the great wall of Babylon was built, asphalt was used to join the bricks to each other. Asphalt was also used to seal the joints of ships. The Bible story of the great flood says that Noah sealed the joints of the ark with *pitch,* another name for asphalt. In Egypt, one use for asphalt was for embalming mummies.

The fact that oil can burn was discovered early. The ancient Hebrews used oil to start the fire on the altar in their temple. The Romans used oil lamps to provide light. The Greeks even used oil in warfare, to set enemy ships on fire.

The ancient Chinese went far beyond merely using petroleum that they found on the surface of the ground. Over 2,200 years ago they drilled for oil, going as deep as 3,000 feet to find it. Their drill bits were made of bronze, the first hard metal of which tools were made. The bits were mounted on rods of bamboo.

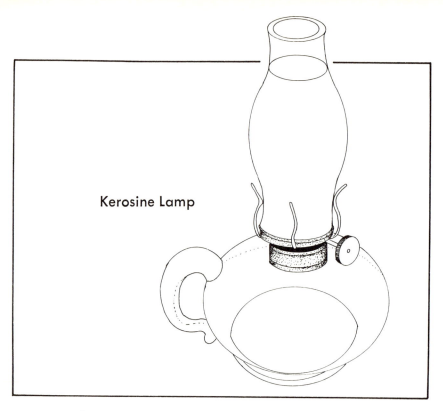

Kerosine Lamp

The Kerosine Lamp and the Automobile

Large-scale production and use of crude oil began in the middle of the nineteenth century, following the invention of the kerosine lamp. In the United States before that time, light was produced by burning animal fat, such as *tallow* from which candles were made, or *whale oil* burned in lamps. The kerosine lamp, invented in 1854, created a demand for crude oil, from which kerosine is made. The first oil well drilled to meet this demand was a 69-foot well, drilled in 1859, in Titusville, Pennsylvania.

Crude oil production was given an even greater boost by the invention of the automobile, powered by an engine that burns *gasoline,* another crude oil product. The first "horseless carriage" with a gasoline engine was built in 1892 by Frank and Charles Duryea. In 1908 Henry Ford began to produce the Model T, the first automobile that was cheap enough for many people to buy it. The need for gasoline and for other petroleum products described on the next page has grown since then, and world production of crude oil has also grown very rapidly to meet this need. In 1911, world production of crude oil was 300 million barrels. (A barrel is 42 United States gallons.) In 1972, world production of crude oil was 18 thousand million barrels, or sixty times as much.

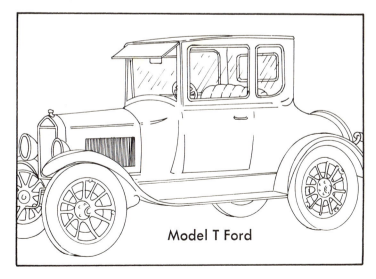

Model T Ford

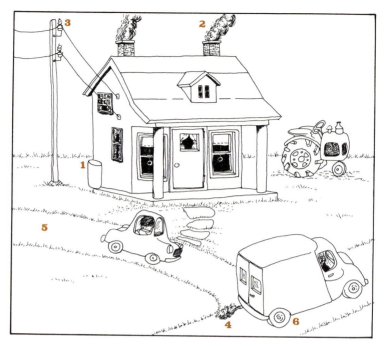

(1) the gas for cooking; (2) the fuel oil that heats the home and (3) powers the electric generator; (4) the gasoline and oil for the car, truck and tractor; (5) the asphalt of the pavement; and (6) the rubber of the tires, all come from crude oil.

Other Uses of Petroleum

The gasoline engine, originally developed for the automobile, now also supplies power for other machines such as trucks, airplanes, buses and farm machinery. The diesel engine, using diesel oil, powers trucks and locomotives. This has further increased the demand for crude oil, from which gasoline and diesel oil are made.

After 1918, when the number of automobiles and trucks used began increasing rapidly, it became necessary to build paved roads for them to ride on. Asphalt became important as a material from which a smooth pavement could be made. At first, the asphalt was taken from asphalt pits. Now most of the asphalt used is made from crude oil.

In automobiles, and in other machines that have moving parts, it is necessary to oil the parts that rub against each other. The lubricating oils used for this purpose are also made from crude oil.

Another important oil produced from crude oil is fuel oil. It is used to heat homes, offices and factories, and to supply power for the steam turbines that turn the generators in many electric power plants. Crude oil is also the raw material from which many chemicals, known as *petrochemicals,* are made. (See pages 36–39.)

Natural gas, found in some oil wells, is used in home heating and cooking, and is also used in industry.

In 1972 the energy consumed in the United States was about 70,000 million million British Thermal Units. (One British Thermal Unit is the amount of heat needed to raise the temperature of one pound of water one degree on the Fahrenheit scale.) Oil and natural gas supplied over three-fourths of this energy.

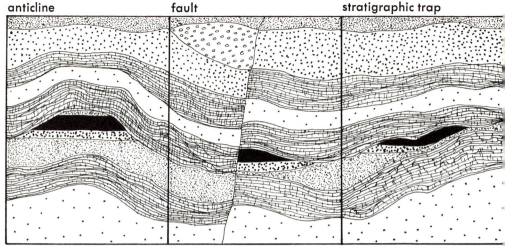

anticline   fault   stratigraphic trap

Three Underground Conditions Which Form
a Trap for Oil

 nonporous ro

Underground Pools of Oil

Oil is lighter than water. For this reason, when oil and ground water are together in porous rocks, the oil floats on top of the water. When the level of the ground water rises, the oil rises with it. If there is only porous rock above the oil, the oil can keep rising until it reaches the surface of the ground. This has happened in some places.

In most places where there is oil in the ground, the rising oil reaches a layer of nonporous rock before it reaches the surface. The oil cannot seep through the rock that is not porous, so it remains under this layer. Under some conditions, the oil is also surrounded on all sides by nonporous rock, so it cannot flow sideways.

Then, unable to rise anymore or flow sideways, the oil is trapped in an underground pool.

Three underground conditions which can form a trap for oil are shown in the drawings on page 14. In the first, called an *anticline*, the layers of rock are folded to form a bump. The nonporous layer above the oil also surrounds it on all sides. In the second, called a *fault*, there is a crack in the ground, and the rock on one side of the crack has slid upward along the crack. The layer of nonporous rock nearest to the oil is separated into two parts. One part is above the oil, and stops it from seeping higher. The other part is alongside the oil, and stops it from flowing sideways. In the third condition, called a *stratigraphic* trap, two layers of nonporous rock, one above the oil and one below it, come together to trap it in a dead end.

Natural gas is lighter than oil. Where there is natural gas in the ground together with the oil, the gas tends to rise above the oil, just as the oil tends to rise above the water. Where the oil is trapped under nonporous rock, the gas is trapped above the oil while the water pushes up against the oil from below. The pressure from the rising water and oil compresses the gas and builds up a back pressure. For this reason there is a high pressure in the gas that is trapped above the oil.

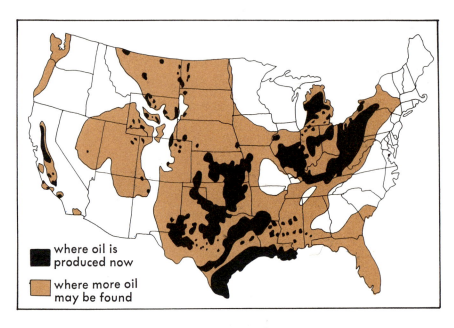

Oil in the United States

After the first oil well was drilled in Pennsylvania, in 1859, the hunt for oil spread throughout the United States. Oil was found in Colorado in 1862, in Texas in 1866, in West Virginia and California in 1875 and in Ohio and Illinois in 1880. During the first part of the twentieth century, oil was discovered in Oklahoma (1905), Louisiana (1906) and Kansas (1916).

California was the leading oil producer from 1903 to 1906. From 1907 to 1928 it was sometimes displaced as leader by Oklahoma. In 1928 Texas moved ahead, and has remained the leading oil-producing state ever since.

An important new discovery was made, in 1938, that there is oil under the continental shelf just off the coast of the United States. The first offshore oil well drilled was in the Gulf of Mexico, one mile off the coast of Louisiana. By 1971, offshore oil from the Gulf coast and the California coast supplied over one-sixth of the crude oil and natural gas used in the United States.

Since 1968, Alaska has joined the list of oil-producing states. The oil field discovered then near Prudhoe Bay, 390 miles north of Fairbanks, is the largest in the Western Hemisphere. It contains about 10 thousand million barrels of crude oil and about 26 million million cubic feet of natural gas. Great as this supply is, it is equal to only about what the United States consumes in two years. In 1972, the United States consumed 5 thousand million barrels of oil and about 23 million million cubic feet of natural gas.

The Oil of the World

Oil fields have been found in many parts of the world. Most of the underground oil is in three oil-rich regions. One of them is the Caribbean Sea and countries bordering on it, such as the United States, Mexico and Venezuela. Another is the Middle East, including the Arabian countries and southern Russia. The third is North Africa.

In 1972, the total amount of oil known to be underground was about 560 thousand million barrels. The Middle East had about 330 thousand million barrels, or more than half of it. The United States had 36 thousand million barrels, or about one-sixteenth of the world supply.

Although the United States doesn't have the largest oil supply in the ground, it produces and uses more oil than any other country. In 1972 it produced 3½ thousand million barrels. The next largest producers were the U.S.S.R., producing almost 3 thousand million barrels, and Saudi Arabia, producing 2¼ thousand million barrels. However, all the Arabian countries together produced twice as much as the United States. The amount produced in a year by each country or region is shown by the black semicircles in the map on page 19.

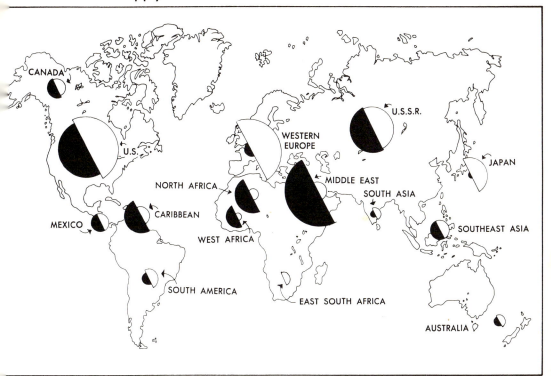

Oil is not always used where it is produced. The amount used in a year in each country or region is shown by the white semicircles in the map. The Middle East uses only a small part of the oil it produces, and sells the rest. Japan and Western Europe produce very little of the oil they use. They buy most of it from the Middle East. The United States used about 5 thousand million barrels in 1972, although it produced only 3½ thousand million barrels. It had to buy the other 1½ thousand million barrels from other countries.

19

Locating Oil

As the oil in known oil fields is pumped out and used up, new oil fields have to be found. The search for oil is guided by past experience.

Past experience shows that oil is found only in layers of rock formed of mud, sand or shells piled up under ancient seas. This type of rock is called *sedimentary* rock. So the first step in a search for oil is to examine geological maps to locate a region where the underground rocks are sedimentary.

Past experience shows that oil is most likely to be found in sandstone or limestone. So, after a region of sedimentary rock is chosen, the second step in a search for oil is to study the ground there, to look for clues

Using an Explosion
to Locate Oil

that show that there is sandstone or limestone underground.

Past experience shows that oil is usually found in traps of the kind described on pages 14 and 15. So the third step is to look for signs on the surface that there may be an oil trap underground.

The fourth step is to try to "see" what is underground before trying to drill a well. This is done with the help of certain instruments. With the *magnetometer*, the geologist measures how the earth's magnetism changes from place to place on the ground. The magnetism is weaker in sedimentary rocks than in other rocks. Another instrument, the *gravimeter*, measures how the pull of gravity changes from place to place on the ground. The pull from sedimentary rocks is weaker than from other rocks. The geologist can also "see" how the rocks underground are arranged in layers, and can "see" folds, faults and crossings in the layers by setting off small explosions in the ground, and then recording the vibrations of the ground with a *seismograph*.

These four steps tell the geologist where oil *may* be. The fifth step, which tells for sure whether oil is really there, is to drill a well. Oil is actually found in only one well out of ten. Commercially usable amounts of oil are found in only one well out of fifty.

Drilling for Oil on Land

Most drilling for oil is done by *rotary drilling* in which the *bit* that cuts into the rock is *rotated* or turned.

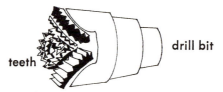

teeth   drill bit

The bit is a short section of pipe with two or three cones mounted at the end. The cones have teeth on them. As the bit turns, the cones roll on the ground, and the teeth bite into the rock and grind it into powder.

The bit is screwed into the end of a long *drill pipe* made up of sections of pipe that are joined by being screwed into a coupling. As the hole made by the drill grows deeper, new sections are joined to the drill pipe.

The top of the drill pipe is screwed into a square-shaped pipe called a *kelly*. The kelly passes through a square hole in a *turntable*. As the turntable is turned by an engine, it makes the kelly turn. Then the drill pipe, since it is attached to the kelly, also turns, and the bit bites into the ground. As the drill pipe descends into the hole, the kelly slides down in the square hole of the turntable.

While the drilling goes on, a special kind of mud is pumped into the drill pipe. The mud goes down the inside of the pipe to the bottom of the well. Then it rises between the outside of the pipe and the rock wall of the well. The mud serves several purposes: It lubricates the drill bit and cools it; it raises to the top the ground-up rock; it keeps ground water from seeping into the well; and it plasters over weak spots in the wall of the well.

At some levels of the deepening well, the wall may need stronger support than the mud alone can give it. Then a wide pipe, called a casing, is lowered into the well and cemented into place. The drill pipe is then lowered into the casing to continue the drilling.

A casing is also put in at the surface. Above this casing is a series of valves that can be closed. They are called *blowout preventers,* and are closed if necessary to stop an uncontrolled flow of oil from the well.

After the drilling is done, more casings are cemented in place as a lining for the well.

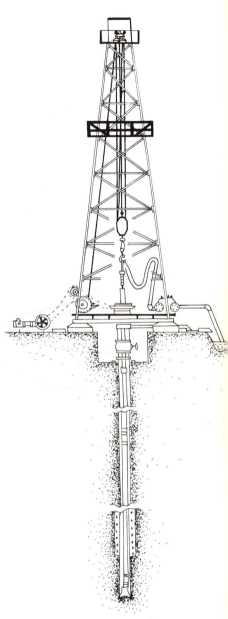

A Rotary Type Drilling Rig

Drilling for Oil at Sea

Offshore drilling is done from a platform, held in place above the spot on the sea floor where the well is to be drilled. The platform may be the top of a tower standing on the sea floor, or it may be the surface of a ship held in place by anchors and cables, and steadied by propellers.

Some towers are built with a platform at one end and a barge at the other end. The tower, lying on its side, is towed to the drilling site. Then the barge end is made to sink to the sea floor. The platform end is supported at the surface by the rest of the tower structure below it.

Some platforms are made with legs that can be raised and lowered. The platform, with legs in the raised position, is towed to the drilling site. There the legs are lowered until they rest on the sea floor.

At first, offshore drilling was possible only in water that was less than 300 feet deep. Now, with improved equipment, it is possible to drill in water that is more than a thousand feet deep.

A Drilling Platform Being Towed

A Drilling Rig in Use in the North Sea

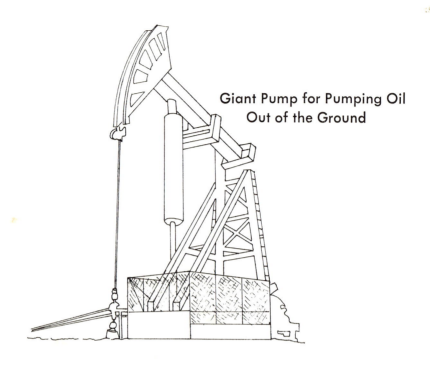

Giant Pump for Pumping Oil
Out of the Ground

Bringing Oil to the Surface

The bottom of an oil well is separated from the pool of oil that surrounds it by the casing, the cement around the casing and even some rock. It is necessary to open up passages through which the oil can flow into the casing. One way of doing this is to lower into the well a special instrument that fires steel bullets through the casing, cement and surrounding rock. The oil and gas, once they start flowing into the well, are brought to the top in tubing that is lowered into the casing.

In a well that has natural gas as well as oil, there is some gas dissolved in the oil, and there may be some outside the oil but trapped and compressed in the space above it. In either case, the gas is under high pressure. Then, when the valves in the tubing are open, the gas pressure forces the oil up and out, the way gas pressure forces soda out of a soda bottle.

There is usually also water under the oil. The water, too, is under high pressure, and is able to push the oil up the tubing.

After a well has been flowing for a long time, the pressure of the gas or water falls, and the flow slows down or stops. Then pumps have to be used to bring the oil to the surface.

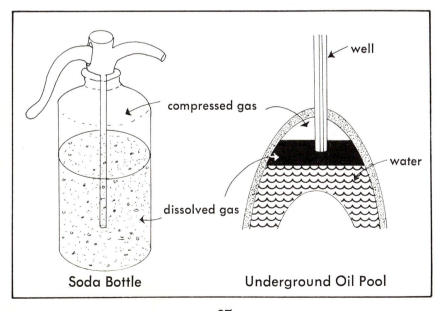

compressed gas

well

water

dissolved gas

Soda Bottle   Underground Oil Pool

What Is in Petroleum

Petroleum is a mixture of many different chemical compounds. Some of the compounds, called *hydrocarbons,* contain only hydrogen and carbon. Others contain, in addition, other elements such as oxygen, nitrogen or sulfur.

Each compound is made up of units called *molecules.* Each molecule is made up of *atoms.* In a hydrocarbon molecule there are only hydrogen atoms and carbon atoms joined together by *bonds.* It is as if each atom has one or more hands with which it can grasp a hand of another atom to form a bond. A carbon atom can form four bonds. A hydrogen atom can form only one bond. In the diagrams of molecules shown on pages 29 and 31, C stands for a carbon atom, H stands for a hydrogen atom and a straight line stands for a bond.

In some hydrocarbon molecules found in petroleum, the carbon atoms are joined to each other in a straight chain, like people in a line holding hands. Each carbon atom, except those at the end of the chain, is joined to two other carbon atoms, one on each side of it. Each carbon atom at the end of the chain is joined to only one other carbon atom. In addition, each carbon atom is joined to enough hydrogen atoms to use up the four

The First Four Paraffins

methane	$\begin{array}{c} H \\ | \\ H-C-H \\ | \\ H \end{array}$
ethane	$\begin{array}{c} H \quad H \\ | \quad | \\ H-C-C-H \\ | \quad | \\ H \quad H \end{array}$
propane	$\begin{array}{c} H \quad H \quad H \\ | \quad | \quad | \\ H-C-C-C-H \\ | \quad | \quad | \\ H \quad H \quad H \end{array}$
butane	$\begin{array}{c} H \quad H \quad H \quad H \\ | \quad | \quad | \quad | \\ H-C-C-C-C-H \\ | \quad | \quad | \quad | \\ H \quad H \quad H \quad H \end{array}$

bonds it can make. Where there is only one carbon atom in the molecule, it is joined to four hydrogen atoms. These straight-chain molecules are called *paraffins*. The four paraffins with the fewest carbon atoms per molecule—methane, ethane, propane and butane—are shown in the diagram on page 29. They are found in natural gas. The paraffin that has eight carbon atoms per molecule is called *octane*.

Some hydrocarbon molecules have two or more straight chains joined to each other to form a branched chain. An example of a branched-chain molecule is shown on page 31. Notice that, like butane, it has four carbon atoms and ten hydrogen atoms, but in this molecule they are arranged differently. For this reason it is called *isobutane*.

In some hydrocarbon molecules, called *naphthenes*, the carbon atoms are joined together to form a closed ring. The example shown on page 31 is called *cyclohexane*.

The hydrocarbon molecules described above are only the simplest of them. Petroleum also contains more complicated molecules, in some of which there are rings joined to rings.

Most of the weight of a molecule is contributed by its carbon atoms. The more carbon atoms a molecule has, the heavier it is. At ordinary temperatures, the heaviest hydrocarbon compounds are solids, the lightest are gases and the rest are liquids. If the solids are made hot enough, they melt into liquids. If the liquids are made hot enough, they evaporate into gases.

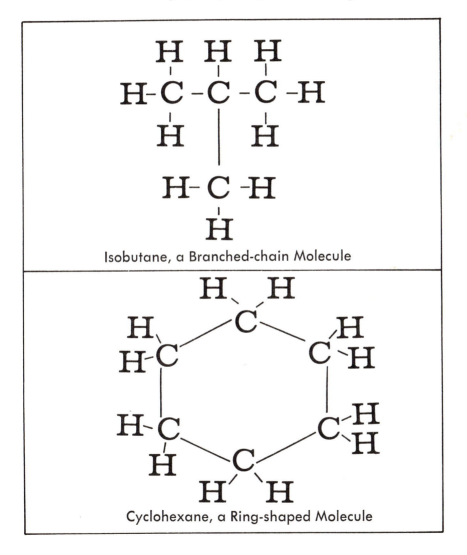

Isobutane, a Branched-chain Molecule

Cyclohexane, a Ring-shaped Molecule

Refining Oil

Gasoline is a mixture of hydrocarbons that have from five to eleven carbon atoms in each molecule. It is produced from crude oil at refineries in three different ways. In one process the gasoline that is in crude oil is separated from the other parts of the crude oil by *fractional distillation*. Gasoline is also produced by *cracking*, which makes gasoline molecules from larger, heavier hydrocarbon molecules by breaking them into pieces. A third process, called *polymerization,* makes gasoline molecules from smaller, lighter ones, by joining them together.

In fractional distillation, crude oil is heated so that it boils to produce a hot vapor. Then the vapor is allowed to rise in a closed tower, and the vapor cools as it rises. As the vapor cools, it begins to condense into a liquid, but the heavier molecules condense first, near the bottom of the tower, where the temperature is higher. The lighter molecules condense later, near the top of the tower, where the temperature is lower. The drops of liquid that form are caught in trays, which are stacked inside the tower, and flow from the trays through pipes. The heaviest liquid, which flows out at the bottom of the tower, is asphalt or heavy fuel oil. The lighter liquids, flowing out at successively higher

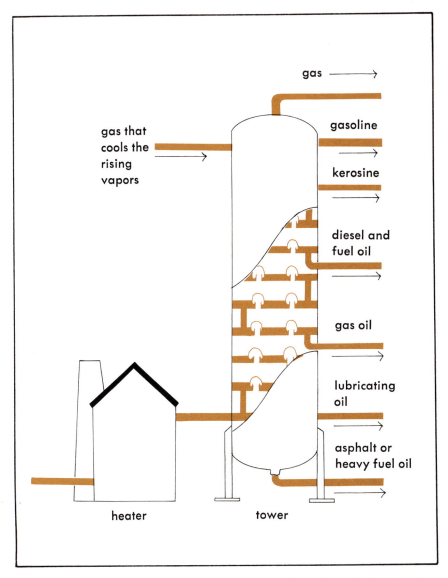

gas ⟶

gas that
cools the
rising
vapors

gasoline

kerosine

diesel and
fuel oil

gas oil

lubricating
oil

asphalt or
heavy fuel oil

heater

tower

levels, are lubricating oil, gas oil, diesel and fuel oil, kerosine and gasoline. The vapor that doesn't condense at all flows out of the top as a gas.

A Tank Truck and Railroad Tank Car

Transporting Gas, Oil and Oil Products

Natural gas has to be sent from the oil and gas fields where it is taken out of the ground to the factories and cities where it is used. Most of it is sent through pipelines. In 1971, there were 915,000 miles of natural gas pipelines in the United States. This is almost four times the distance from here to the moon.

Crude oil has to be taken from the oil fields to the refineries. Then the products of the refineries have to be taken to the places where they are used. Oil and oil products are carried overland by pipelines, railroad tank cars and tank trucks. They are carried across the sea in ocean tankers, and on lakes and rivers in barges.

In the United States there are 218,000 miles of pipeline for carrying crude oil and liquid oil products. One of these pipelines carries gasoline from Texas to New York. Another one will be built to bring oil from Alaska to the other states. The oil is pushed through a pipeline by pumps spaced out along the line about 50 to 150 miles apart. The oil moves through the line at a speed of two or three miles per hour.

The largest ocean tankers are more than 1,100 feet long, and can carry up to 2¾ million barrels of oil at a time.

An Oil Tanker

Petrochemicals

Petroleum is not only a source of fuels like gasoline, kerosine and fuel oil. It is also the raw material for making thousands of useful products, including such different things as rubber, paints, rayon, explosives, food containers, antifreeze and phonograph records.

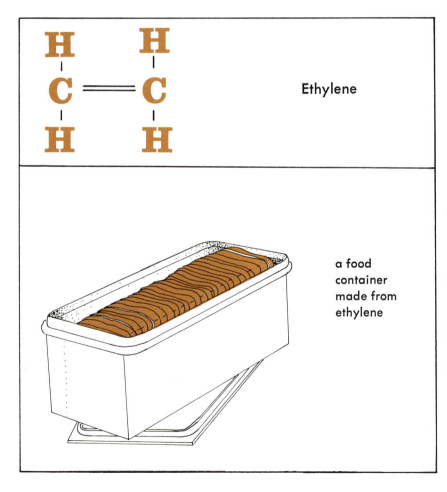

Ethylene

a food container made from ethylene

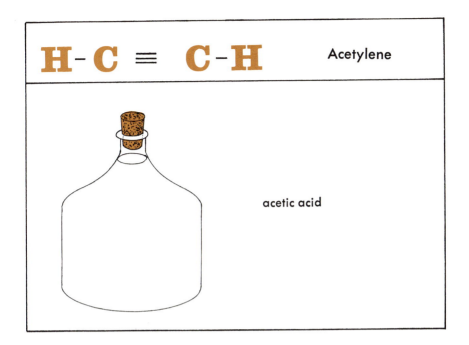

$$H-C \equiv C-H$$ Acetylene

acetic acid

The first step toward making these products is to produce certain petrochemicals, each of which has many uses.

The single most important petrochemical is *ethylene*, a gas which has two carbon atoms in each molecule. Some ethylene is produced when petroleum is cracked, and more of it is made from ethane and propane. Ethylene is used to make polyethylene, from which food containers are made, and vinyl chloride, from which phonograph records and garden hoses are made. It is also used to make rubber and antifreeze. Ethyl alcohol, which used to be made only from grain or molasses, is now made from ethylene, too.

Some Products Made from Petrochemicals

rayon dress

phonograph record

paint

garden hose

antifreeze

plastic seat cover

rubber tire

Another important two-carbon petrochemical is *acetylene*. It used to be made only from coal. Now it is made from methane. Products made from acetylene include acetic acid (the acid in vinegar), acetate fiber, vinyl chloride and vinyl acetate, from which plastics and adhesives are made.

Propylene is a three-carbon petrochemical. Some of it is a product of the cracking process, and more of it is made from propane. Propylene products include detergents, used for washing, and isopropyl alcohol, used as an antifreeze and for making acetone. Acetone, which used to be made only from wood, is used to make explosives, airplane "dopes," and rayon.

Butylene is a four-carbon petrochemical from which rubber is made.

Benzene is a six-carbon petrochemical in whose molecules the six carbon atoms form a closed ring. Benzene used to be made only from coal, but now it is made from petroleum, too. It is used as a solvent, as a fuel and as a raw material for making other products.

Toluene is a seven-carbon ring petrochemical. It is the chemical from which the explosive TNT is made.

Xylene is an eight-carbon ring petrochemical used for making paints and plastics, and the fiber that is called Dacron in the United States and Terylene in England.

Our use of oil produces many good results. It gives us energy for heating our homes and running our machines. And it gives us many useful petrochemical products. But not all the results of using oil are good. One of the bad results is *pollution,* a spoiling of the ground and sea, and especially of the air.

When oil is carried across the sea in tankers, and when offshore wells are drilled at sea, there is sometimes an accident, and oil is spilled. The spilled oil floating on the water kills fish and birds. If it is washed up on shore, it dirties beaches and makes them unfit for use. The danger of oil spills creates the problem of finding ways of preventing them from happening and of cleaning up the oil quickly and thoroughly when they do happen.

When oil is burned in a furnace and when gasoline is burned in an automobile engine, some gases are produced that dirty the air. One of these gases is *carbon monoxide,* which is poisonous. Some of the gases are hydrocarbons that can make people ill. Large amounts of hydrocarbon in the air of big cities make a *smog* that irritates the eyes and lungs, and may cut off as much as one-fourth of the sunlight. Some fuel oils contain *sulfur*. When these oils are burned, the air

Dead Oil-soaked Bird
Santa Barbara Beach, February 1969

is dirtied by sulfur dioxide, which hurts people and damages clothing, paint and metal. Some gasoline in the past contained *lead*, which was put into it to prevent knocking in the engine. But, when gasoline with lead is burned, the lead is put into the air that people breathe, and lead is a dangerous poison. So, burning fuel oil and gasoline creates the problem of trying to do it in a way that dirties the air as little as possible. In the United States, there are now laws forbidding the burning of oil that has a lot of sulfur and of gasoline that contains lead. Other laws require that automobile makers reduce the amount of harmful gases a new automobile puts into the air.

How Long Will Oil Last?

The oil we take out of the ground was made by nature millions of years ago. It is not replaced as we use it up, and we use it at a faster rate every year. Some time in the future it will all be gone, burned up in our furnaces and automobiles. When will that be?

To answer this question it is necessary to know how much oil there is in the ground, and how fast it is being used.

In the United States in 1972, the amount of oil known to be in the ground in oil fields already discovered was about 36 thousand million barrels. The oil was being taken out of the ground and used at the rate of 3½ thousand million barrels a year. At this rate, the known oil supply in the United States would be used up in eleven years. However, new oil fields are being discovered every year. The oil in them will last, at most, another 120 years.

In 1972, the world supply of oil in oil fields already discovered was 560 thousand million barrels, and it was being used at the rate of 18½ thousand million barrels a year. At this rate the known world supply of oil will last only thirty years. The discovery of more fields is likely to extend the time another thirty or forty years at most.

The World's Energy

Energy is used when people work to produce food, clothing, houses and other useful things. Rich countries, which produce and use much, use up a lot of energy. Poor countries, which produce and use little, use a smaller amount of energy. A large part of the energy used comes from burning fuels made from oil.

The richest countries of the world are the United States, the U.S.S.R., Japan and the countries of Western Europe. In 1972, together they had only one-fourth of the world's population, but they used two-thirds of the world's oil. The United States alone had only one-eighteenth of the world's population, but it used one-fourth of the world's oil.

But the poorer countries are now building more factories and railroads, and are beginning to use more automobiles and trucks. This means that they will be using more and more oil each year. As the poorer countries begin to use a larger share of the world's oil, the richer countries will have to use a smaller share. Meanwhile, as world industry and population grow, the world's limited oil supply will be used up faster and faster. There will be a shortage of oil during the next thirty years throughout the world, and especially in the United States.

In 1972, the United States bought one-fourth of the oil it used from other countries. In future years it will have to rely less on oil imported from abroad and more on oil produced at home. To make the home supply of oil last as long as possible, it is necessary to conserve or save oil as much as possible.

An oil well flows as long as the pressure in it is strong enough to push the oil up. When the pressure is lost, there is usually still some oil left in the ground. We can save oil by bringing some of this leftover oil up. One way of doing this is to pump water into the oil well. Another way is to space wells at the same field far enough apart so that they do not reduce the pressure too fast. The oil companies are also trying to find new ways of bringing up more oil.

We can also save oil by using less of it. On the road, we can save gasoline and the oil from which it is made by driving no faster than 55 miles per hour. We can save more by using small cars instead of large cars. And we can save still more by using buses and trains more and using private cars less. In factories we can save oil by switching back to coal as a fuel. At home we can save oil by not overheating our homes and by not wasting electricity.

Oil for the Future

As we use up the supply of oil that is in the oil fields already discovered, it is necessary to find a new supply for the future. A part of this supply will come from new oil fields that will be discovered during the next ten or twenty years. But the oil in these fields, too, will be used up in a short time. Fortunately, there are other ways of getting oil besides pumping it out of an underground pool.

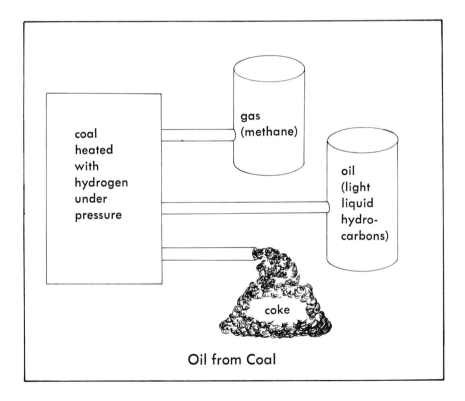

Oil from Coal

In a few places there are deposits of sand and clay that are gummy with oil. These deposits are called *tar sands*. The oil can be removed from tar sands by washing it out with hot water. There is enough tar sand in Canada to supply 400 thousand million barrels of oil.

In many countries there are large amounts of a rock called *oil shale*. Oil shale contains *kerogen,* which, like petroleum, consists of the remains of small plants and animals that lived in ancient seas or lakes. If oil shale is mined, crushed and heated, the process produces *shale oil* from the kerogen. Shale oil can be refined to produce gasoline, kerosine, diesel fuel and jet fuel. One ton of the best oil shale can yield as much as one hundred gallons of shale oil. It is estimated that the oil shale of the Rocky Mountains can supply about 2 million million barrels of shale oil. This is over 50 times the oil supply still in the oil fields that have been found in the United States.

There are also ways of making oil from *coal*. Studies are now being made to find the best and cheapest methods of doing it. There are about 1½ million million tons of coal in the ground in the United States. About one-third of this amount can be mined and will probably be the raw material out of which most of the oil of the future will be made in the United States.

Index